BETTER UNDERSTAND IDIOMS, PHRASES, AND SAYINGS

And Discover the Fascinating

History Behind Their Origins

C000196284

COOPER THE POOPER

© Copyright 2022 by Cooper the Pooper - All rights reserved.

The content contained within this book may not be reproduced, duplicated or transmitted without direct written permission from the author or the publisher.

Under no circumstances will any blame or legal responsibility be held against the publisher, or author, for any damages, reparation, or monetary loss due to the information contained within this book, either directly or indirectly.

Legal Notice:
This book is copyright protected. It is only for personal use. You cannot amend, distribute, sell, use, quote or paraphrase any part, or the content within this book, without the consent of the author or publisher.

Disclaimer Notice:
Please note the information contained within this document is for educational and entertainment purposes only. All effort has been executed to present accurate, up to date, reliable, complete information. No warranties of any kind are declared or implied. Readers acknowledge that the author is not engaged in the rendering of legal, financial, medical or professional advice. The content within this book has been derived from various sources. Please consult a licensed professional before attempting any techniques outlined in this book.

By reading this document, the reader agrees that under no circumstances is the author responsible for any losses, direct or indirect, that are incurred as a result of the use of the information contained within this document, including, but not limited to, errors, omissions, or inaccuracies.

TABLE OF CONTENTS

INTRODUCTION

The English language contains hundreds of thousands of words. We use them to say, write, and sign things, every day. We put them together in common, unique, predictable, and even strange ways. Sometimes a particular string of words is so interesting, fun, smart, or otherwise remarkable enough that it sticks around. We reuse a phrase and others start to use it, and then it spreads.

Sometimes it will only become part of the slang of a certain generation, or the dialect of a specific area. Other times, it becomes part of the basics of English and is taught to children beside fundamental grammar. Often, it is not even taught. It simply is. Do you remember when you learned that the blue thing above us is the sky? Where did you learn that "when pigs fly" means never? People around us use a saying and, because it is what is said, we use it as well.

But – have you ever wondered, what does that mean?

Some things we say are pretty straightforward in their meaning, but others seem strange. Some idioms and expressions are a few decades old; others are hundreds of years old. A few of the phrases we use today are similar to ones that were used thousands of years ago, but in Latin and Greek. Most of our newer sayings come from America, whereas the older ones are from England. In this book, you'll find sayings that are used in American and British English, and even some that seem to hop back and forth across the Atlantic.

Now, I'm sure you're eager to jump straight in with "a bull in a china shop," but "hang on a minute." Just in case you are wondering, what is an expression, an idiom, and a saying? Is there even a difference between them? Let's look at that before we "jump in with both feet".

A saying is a sentence or phrase that is catchy and commonly used. There are dozens of different types of sayings. These include clichés, mottos, proverbs, expressions, idioms, and many other things.

An expression is a saying that has a fairly straightforward meaning.

An idiom is an expression that you mustn't take literally. You won't know what an idiom means just by knowing what each word in the phrase means. With an idiom, you have to understand something about the *implied* meaning of the phrase.

A BULL IN A CHINA SHOP

"There wasn't any milk, so Amy asked Uncle Jake if he could put a little less chili in the stew; but like **A BULL IN A CHINA SHOP**, she managed to seriously offend him! Now he refuses to cook when we visit.**"**

 Being physically clumsy, or dealing with a sensitive situation clumsily.

 When porcelain was first imported to Europe, from China, they called it Chinaware. Over time, Europeans shortened this to 'china'.

The idiom, bull in a china shop, first appeared in poetry in the 1800s. Two songs, one from 1805 and one from 1808, had the idiom as their titles. This led researchers to suspect that the phrase started out purely as vivid imagery.

However, consider the fact that one of London's oldest markets, Old Spitalfields, opened in 1638. Additionally, millions of cattle and other animals were driven on hoof through the city streets to the London cattle markets, until 1939. England started importing porcelain in the middle of the 1600s. This means that, although there is no evidence that this situation ever literally happened, all the elements were in place. Perhaps it did happen but was not written about in any newspaper or in any book that we can find today. Maybe an angry bull in the market was simply a market stall owner's worst fear.

An older variation of this idiom exists; "donkey in a potter's shop," and it was used about 2400 years ago. The Greek storyteller, Aesop, used the phrase in one of his fables. He, of course, did not write it in English.

A LITTLE BIRD TOLD ME

"A LITTLE BIRD TOLD ME that you were spotted on a date with that cute guy you were talking about the other day! Tell me everything. How was it?**"**

 MEANING Someone—but I will not say who—told me a piece of news or gossip.

Homing pigeons were used to send messages, from as early as a thousand years ago. Although it is a lot less common these days, small items and messages are still occasionally carried by birds. In ancient times, the message would be rolled up and put in a tube tied to a pigeon's feet. In more modern times, a small satchel is sometimes placed around the shoulders of the bird instead.

The idiom has been in use since 1546. It might have started with people literally receiving messages carried by birds, who only said that they got news from a bird, rather than revealing who had sent the pigeon's message.

There are also various legends and fairy-tales about birds telling heroes secrets, such as the location of a treasure or their enemy's weakness. These stories may have inspired people to say "a bird told me" as a way to say that something is a secret.

Today, people will often use a diminutive form and say, "a little birdie told me." This may be inspired by popular fairy-tale movie adaptions in the late 1900s and early 2000s.

A PIECE OF CAKE

"I studied really hard last night.
This test should be **A PIECE OF CAKE."**

 Something is super easy.

 This idiom stems from another, older idiom with the same meaning: "cakewalk," which is also used to describe very simple tasks.

During the time of slavery in America, white slave owners would often put on entertainment spectacles. They were originally called "Prize Walks" and later, "Cakewalks." During them, black couples would perform intricate dance moves and the winning couple received either a whole cake, or a piece of a cake. It is speculated that the black couple may occasionally have exaggerated their dancing in ways that mocked upper-class white society. The white judges, of course, were oblivious. By the 1870s, after slavery had been abolished, cakewalks were heavily featured in minstrel shows and the name was cemented in memory.

Exactly why the cakewalk and, subsequently, desserts such as cake and pie became synonymous with doing something easy remains unclear. Cakewalks were, after all, fairly intricate and difficult. Still, the cakewalk idiom was in use for many years before "piece of cake" overtook it in the 1930s.

Perhaps having less cake was easier after all.

ADD FUEL TO THE FIRE

66Why do you always have to **ADD FUEL TO THE FIRE**?
We were already in trouble,
but then you just had to be sarcastic to him!**99**

MEANING Make something worse than it already is.

ORIGIN We know the Latin version of this expression existed as far back as 1 AD as a Roman historian, Livius, used it in a history book that he wrote then. It is easy to see how the expression jumped from literal to figurative. If a house is on fire, you do not want to throw more flammable material onto it. If a situation is bad, you do not want to add anything that makes it worse.

The expressions "digging yourself a hole," "out of the frying pan and into the fire," and "up the creek without a paddle" also mean a bad situation that is not likely to get better.

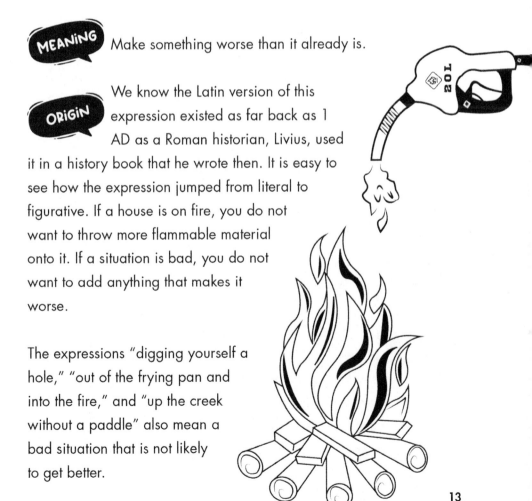

ALL THUMBS

"I really did try my best to make a good clay pot, but I'm not much of an artist. To tell the truth, I'm **ALL THUMBS** when it comes to any sort of craft project.**"**

 MEANING Having poor physical dexterity or useless, clumsy, unskilled hands.

ORIGIN "All thumbs" was first recorded as part of a 1546 proverb by John Heywood: "When he should get aught, each finger is a thumb." In this case, *aught* meant *everything*, even though it eventually came to mean *nothing*. Opposable thumbs are extremely useful. However, this phrase is meant to show how awkward it would be to hold anything if *all* your fingers were thumbs.

ANTS IN ONE'S PANTS

"Do you have to go to the bathroom or something? You've been so jumpy all night it looks as if you've got **ANTS IN YOUR PANTS."**

MEANING To be stressed, tightly wound up, or constantly moving around energetically.

ORIGIN This idiom comes from a 1930s jingle, "I Can't Dance (I've Got Ants in My Pants)" by Roy Newman. A shortened version, "you look antsy," has been in use since the 1960s.

Other expressions with the same meaning include "being on the edge of one's seat" and "being on tenterhooks." However, "having ants in your pants" is definitely the most colorful and fun of these.

AS EASY AS ABC

66Pour two tablespoons of oil into a pot on the stove, throw a cup of popcorn kernels in, cover with a lid and wait until there is a 3-second pause between pops. See, making popcorn is **AS EASY AS ABC.**99

 MEANING Very simple and easy.

 ORIGIN One of the first things most children learn is the alphabet, or their ABCs. Moreover, A, B, and C are the first letters most children learn. So, the connection between this expression and something being easy is pretty straightforward. The "easy as ABC" version has been used since the 1800s. An earlier form, "as plain as ABC," existed from the 1600s. There are two other expressions in a similar vein: "it's child's play," and "it's as easy as stealing from a baby." Both are similarly clear in meaning, but the latter is perhaps less literally advisable.

AT A SNAIL'S PACE

❝I wish I was the sort of person who could finish reading entire novels in a matter of hours, but unfortunately, I read **AT A SNAIL'S PACE.** I've been working on finishing just one book for over three months now.**❞**

 Very, very slowly.

 On average, snails travel at around sixteen feet an hour (with no pauses). That means a snail could only move about half a mile, even if it moved constantly for a full 24 hours. Very slow indeed!

William Shakespeare seems to have liked the phrase. He used it in two of his plays: *Troilus and Cressida*, which was published in 1609: *"Go, bear Patroclus' body to Achilles"; And bid the snail-paced Ajax arm for shame."*, and *Richard III*, *"Delay leads impotent and snail-paced beggary"*, which was first performed in 1633. Those are the most famous early examples. but the expression itself dates back to the 1400s.

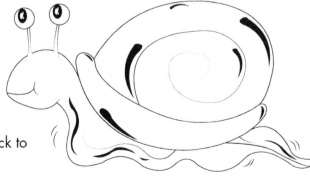

BEE iN ONE'S BONNET

"Sam has had a **BEE IN HIS BONNET** about Greek mythology since he read that book.**"**

MEANING To be obsessed with a specific idea.

ORiGiN A bonnet is a women's hat of soft material with no brim, and which ties under the chin. Women in the 1600s would usually have all their hair caught under their bonnet, with only the fringe showing.

In use since the 1600s, this idiom may be related to the expression "buzzing thoughts." That means to have thoughts flicking through your mind as quickly and distractingly as a hive of annoyed bees. The implication is then that someone is thinking so hard, their thoughts are buzzing as if the person has bees in their head or under their hat. The theory is that this imagery then led to the idiom "bee in her bonnet."

Another theory is that it comes from the image of a person thinking and moving frantically, as if they have a bee in their clothing.

BLOW OFF SOME STEAM

“Man, that rude guy made me so mad. I think I'll go visit the batting cages to **BLOW OFF SOME STEAM.****”**

MEANING To participate in an active, vigorous, or violent activity in order to decrease one's levels of anger or restlessness.

ORIGIN Steam power was heavily used during the 1800s, from trains through steamboats to household items. The mechanism worked when a boiler heated water to the point where it became steam. When this steam built up pressure, it pushed a piston, which caused the motor to move. However, if the pressure get too high, the engineer needed to open what were called "blow valves" to release some of the steam. Otherwise, the entire system could—and in many cases *did*—explode!

The change to a figurative reference to people can easily be seen. How many times have you heard about someone, blowing up in anger or frustration?

19

BURY THE HATCHET

HATCHET
BURIED HERE

"Look, high school was years and years ago, and I'm not angry about what you said anymore. Why don't we **BURY THE HATCHET** and start over?"

 MEANING To forget about a past conflict.

ORIGIN A hatchet is a small axe with a short handle that can be held in one hand. In the past, this and other similar axes were sometimes used as weapons. As part of a peace ceremony between some North American First Nation tribes, the chiefs of both parties may have buried their weapons in the ground, to symbolize an end to the fighting. Sometimes the hatchets would be buried beneath the roots of a white pine, as it is a symbol of great peace to some First Nations tribes.

BUSY AS A BEE

"Every time I see you, you're off handling a different issue around the office. You're as **BUSY AS A BEE!"**

MEANING

To be constantly doing something. Usually applied to work, but can be used to describe an extremely social person as well.

ORIGIN

This phrase was recorded as early as the late 1300s. Geoffrey Chaucer described women with "*In wommen [sic] been! for ay as bisy [sic] as bees*" in his 1392 work, *The Canterbury Tales.*

It is little wonder that bees are considered the ultimate hard workers. Female honeybees, called worker bees, literally work in service of their hive until the moment they die!

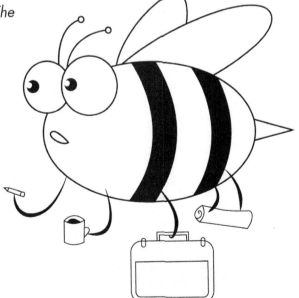

CALL IT A DAY

❝Let's **CALL IT A DAY**, team. We're not going to get anything else done until the client replies to our email anyway.**❞**

MEANING To finish for the time being and leave, even if the work is not done.

ORIGIN This phrase was first noted in 1838, as "call it a half-day." It was used by workers to explain that they wouldn't be staying for the remainder of their shift. The boss would mark them down as having only worked a half-day to keep from paying them their full salary. "Call it a day" was first used in 1919, and "call it a night" was added in 1938. Variations of a similar expression, "Wrap things up for now," seem to be more popular these days.

CAT GOT YOUR TONGUE

66You were so talkative before you realized how wrong
you were. What, **CAT GOT YOUR TONGUE?**99

 MEANING
A sarcastic or threatening way of asking someone why
they've suddenly become speechless.

ORIGIN
When this phrase was first recorded in *Bayou's Monthly*,
an American magazine, it said, "Has the cat got your
tongue, as the children say?". This instantly suggests that
the phrase is actually older than its first written appearance. How
much older, though, remains something of a mystery.

One of the most popular guesses is that the "cat" is actually the cat o' nine-tails, the name of a whip that was used on sailing ships. One might go silent in the face of punishment, or, indeed, after it had been carried out.

Others claim that the expression comes from the idea that witches and their so-called familiars—often black cats—might steal a person's tongue to keep them from reporting on the witches' work.

Lastly, some claim the phrase dates back all the way to Ancient Egypt. There, someone might have their tongue removed for saying something they should not have. The tongue would then be fed to cats. There is evidence of tongues and other body parts being removed as punishment in Ancient Egypt, as recorded in a peace treaty from Ramses II's rule. However, whether those parts were ever given to cats is unclear.

COOL AS A CUCUMBER

66 If I was giving that speech, I'd be terrified! Not that guy, though. He's as **COOL AS A CUCUMBER.** **99**

Remaining perfectly calm, even in the face of great pressure.

I really thought this was going to be a more recent expression, but this metaphor can be traced to John Gay's 1732 poem, *New Song on New Similes*. It contains has the line *"If Molly were but kind; Cool as a cucumber could see, The rest of womankind."*

The word "cool" here refers to an unbothered temperament rather than a temperature. This meaning can be found as far back as *Beowulf*, an Old English epic poem that was written sometime between 700 and 1000 AD. However, the saying was really popularized in Shakespeare's era, the 1600s, when he used it in several of his plays.

You might think that modern slang such as *cool* and *chill* relates to "cool as a cucumber." Yet, it seems that this is descended from 1940s African-American jazz slang, *"cool cat."* Perhaps there is a link between *"cool cat"* and *"cool as a cucumber."* Honestly, it is hard to determine where phrases inspired each other and where things developed independently. Regardless, it seems that being cool and calm has been the in thing for centuries.

CROSS YOUR FINGERS

"CROSS YOUR FINGERS, everyone! They're about to announce the winners!**"**

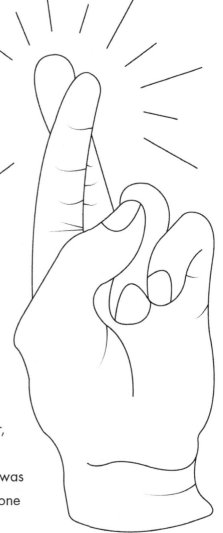

 A gesture used to invoke good luck. Alternatively, crossing one's fingers behind one's back may be used when telling a lie.

 It is said that physically crossing the fingers creates a cross shape and that it was used by persecuted Christians during the 1600s. However, the oldest evidence of the saying only goes back to 1787. In that context, it was used to ward off bad luck when someone walked underneath a ladder.

CRY CROCODILE TEARS

“She's so fake. I know she doesn't care about him at all, but the second he tries to break up with her, she **CRIES CROCODILE TEARS**, and he comes running right back.”

MEANING To force oneself to cry fake tears in an attempt to manipulate others.

ORIGIN This phrase may date back as far as Ancient Egypt, or another ancient culture. It stems from the fact that crocodiles really do cry. The original phrase referred to the way crocs appear to weep while eating their prey, almost making it appear as though they are remorseful for killing other animals.

While crocodiles probably do not truly feel any guilt, some sources claim that the tears appear because they blow large quantities of warm air through their sinuses while eating, which then causes their eyes to well up. Other sources point out that tears are only released when the eye dries out. This would be more visible to humans if a croc was spending a large amount of time on land while eating. Still others claim that the croc cries in order to offset the salt levels in their bodies that come from consuming sodium-rich food.

It is less clear exactly when the phrase moved from a literal to a general meaning. However, in 1603, it was used in Shakespeare's play *Othello* to describe Desdemona's crying, which Othello had been led to believe was insincere: "*If that the earth could teem with woman's tears, Each drop she falls would prove a crocodile.*"

CURIOSITY KILLED THE CAT

"Well, what did he expect, breaking into
an abandoned house that is rumored to be haunted?
CURIOSITY KILLED THE CAT after all."

MEANING Looking too deeply into something, which leads to an unpleasant/disastrous outcome.

ORIGIN In his 1598 play, *Every Man in His Humour*, Ben Jonson first used the line "care will kill a cat." In full, it is: "*Helter skelter, hang sorrow, care'll kill a cat, up-tails all, and a louse for the hangman.*"

The following year, William Shakespeare revisited the phrase in his play *Much Ado About Nothing* with the line "*What, courage man! What though care killed a cat, thou hast mettle enough in thee to kill care.*"

In both cases, the word *care* is synonymous with worry or anxiety, meaning that too much stress will cause a cat to die. It is less clear when the word *curiosity* was substituted for *care*, but by 1837, James Allan Mair's *A Handbook of Proverbs* lists the phrase as "*curiosity killed the cat.*"

By the way! Some people claim that the full original phrase is "Curiosity killed the cat, but satisfaction brought it back"; however this last part was not added until 1912. In 1905, the *Galveston Daily News* published the line "*Curiosity killed a cat; but it came back.*"

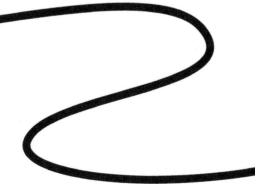

A DIFFERENT KETTLE OF FISH

“Being good at basketball doesn't give you an advantage in football. That's **A WHOLE DIFFERENT KETTLE OF FISH!**”

MEANING This can mean that there is a large difference between two seemingly similar things.

ORIGIN A "fish kettle" was a long, oval-shaped cooking pot used to cook whole salmon, which would then be eaten using one's hands. It is believed a Scottish riverside picnic in the 1700s would be called "a kettle of fish" because the picnic would center around catching and eating fish.

The phrase is first seen in writing from the 1700s. It is a variation on "a pretty kettle of fish," which means things are a mess. This meaning likely came either from how messy the fish-eating process was, or from the confusion of sight and sound caused by a large group of people picnicking together. Finally, a *different* kettle of fish means a situation that is still messy or complicated, but in a different way.

DOGGY BAG

"That was much too much food!
I can't wait to eat this tomorrow. Excuse me, waiter,
may I please have a **DOGGY BAG?"**

MEANING A to-go bag to take home leftover food after dining out at a restaurant.

ORIGIN During World War II, some restaurants began offering bags of table scraps for pet owners to give to their dogs. This happened because food was scarce at the time and it was rationed; so, giving pets scraps from the table helped save on feeding them. At some point, people started asking for bags or boxes of their own leftover food, with the intention of eating it later.

Doggy bag

These days, it is more common for people to ask to have leftovers for "take-away." This may be due to a rising awareness that human food is not great for pets, to the larger food portions we are given, or just because the concept of take-away services has become so common

DON'T PUT ALL OF YOUR EGGS IN ONE BASKET

“You really should consider applying for more than one college. Sure, you'll probably get into your top choice, but **DON'T PUT ALL OF YOUR EGGS IN ONE BASKET.** You should have a fallback option or two just in case.”

 Do not invest all of your time, energy, money, or resources, etc. into just one option.

 Although the expression was probably created earlier, the oldest documented use was in Miguel de Cervantes' 1605 novel, *Don Quixote*. He wrote, "*It is the part of a wise man to keep himself today for tomorrow, and not venture all his eggs in one basket.*" The novel was originally published in Spanish, but was translated into English in 1612.

This expression is also a proverb, as it offers practical advice.

DOWN TO THE WIRE

"We've known about this project for four months already, but he started two days before it was due. He really likes to let things go **DOWN TO THE WIRE**, doesn't he?**"**

 At the last minute.

ORIGIN In horse racing, before there were high-speed cameras, a wire was strung across the finish line to help the officials determine the winner. The figurative use of the wire came into use around the 1900s.

A similar expression, "neck and neck," also comes from horse racing from the 1800s. When two or more horses' necks are near-level with each other, it means that they are so close in speed and proximity that it is nearly impossible to determine who might win. In cases such as this this, when neither horse was clearly ahead, a wire helped to determine things at the end of the race.

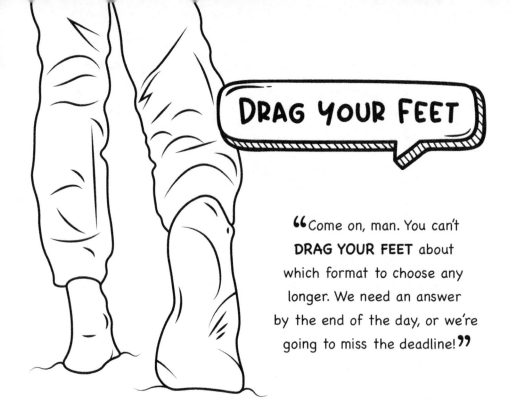

DRAG YOUR FEET

"Come on, man. You can't **DRAG YOUR FEET** about which format to choose any longer. We need an answer by the end of the day, or we're going to miss the deadline!**"**

 To slow or delay work, an outcome, or a decision.

 The phrase "drag your heels" or "drag your feet" can be traced back to the 1940s. It probably came about from someone's observing the physical act of dragging one's feet along the ground in order to slow down something towards which you were moving.

Some other amusing expressions that mean the same include to "filibuster," "shilly-shally," "dillydally," or "lollygag."

DRAW A BLANK

"I've been trying to remember her name for twenty minutes now, but I have to admit I've **DRAWN A BLANK.** **"**

MEANING To try to think of something, but to come up with nothing.

ORIGIN In 1567, Queen Elizabeth I of England implemented a lottery system. Numerous prizes were written on slips of paper and placed in a container to be drawn. Unlike modern lotteries, there were many prizes, including silver plates or tapestries. However, it was still possible to win nothing by drawing a blank slip of paper.

The phrase was also recorded in Washington Irving's 1824 collection of essays and short stories, *Tales of a Traveller*, although at that time the phrase largely meant "to fail at something." It has only recently come to refer exclusively to memory issues rather than all missed opportunities.

DROP THE BALL

"We really **DROPPED THE BALL** on this one, boys.
If we can't at least get *something* together before
the party starts, the boss is going to be really upset.**"**

 MEANING To fail at something, through your own fault.

 ORIGIN The expression was originally only used in sports cases
when a player literally dropped a ball and caused
problems for their team. By the 1950s, its use had been
expanded to cover non-literal situations.

FALL ON DEAF EARS

❝His pleas for peace **FELL ON DEAF EARS**. The people were too angry to stop the commotion.❞

MEANING To have one's words completely ignored.

ORIGIN This phrase was first recorded in a collection of proverbs in 1546 but probably dates back further, to the mid-1400s. There are also a few references to "deaf ears" in the Bible, including the line *"they are like the deaf adder that stoppeth her ear."* Whether that exact phrasing was used prior to the King James edition, translated in 1611, is not something I can be certain of, however.

FILL IN THE BLANKS

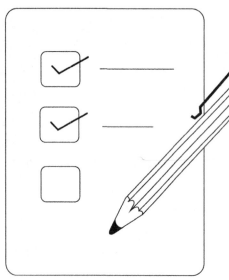

"They haven't assigned me any new projects, and my manager hasn't looked me in the eye in weeks. You **FILL IN THE BLANKS,** it's obvious. And if I'm wrong, please still fill in the blanks for me, because if I'm not being fired, I have no idea what is going on. **"**

 MEANING Make an obvious conclusion, or suggest or provide some missing information. Often used rhetorically, where the speaker does not really expect an answer.

 ORIGIN This phrase originated in the 1800s. It probably came with the rise of printed paperwork that allowed clients, visitors, or office workers to complete forms by just filling in the blanks.

Similar expressions include "put two and two together," "follow the breadcrumbs," "bridge the gaps," and "find the common thread."

FISH OUT OF WATER

"He said he would meet me at the party,
but he didn't show up. I didn't know anyone, so I just stood
around feeling like a **FISH OUT OF WATER.**"

 To be in a situation with which you are unfamiliar and uncomfortable with.

ORIGIN It is rather obvious that few things are as out of place as a fish is on land. This idiom has been in use for centuries. Around 1390, Chaucer wrote in his *Canterbury Tales: Prologue* that *"a monk without a cloister is like a fish without water."* The first modern English version of this saying appears in 1613, in Samuel Perchas' *Purchas his Pilgrimage* as, *"Fishes out of the Water"*.

FOR THE BIRDS

"The lift is broken? Well, they are **FOR THE BIRDS** if they think I'm going to climb thirty flights of stairs!**"**

 MEANING Something that is nonsense.

ORIGIN American soldiers started using the idiom "it's dung for the birds" during the Second World War. It is a reference to the animal dung birds sometimes peck through for seeds to eat, meaning that it was a variation on curses involving bull or horse dung. By 1943, "it's strictly for the birds" was part of teenage slang and by 1944 all ages of people had started using the shorter version, "for the birds."

GET A KICK OUT OF SOMETHING

"That's hilarious! Tell that joke to your dad. He'll definitely **GET A KICK OUT OF IT.""**

MEANING To find enjoyment in something.

ORIGIN In the 1934 American Broadway musical *Anything Goes*, a song by Cole Porter, *I Get a Kick Out of You* is sung. This song popularized the slang meaning of *kick* as well as the saying.

GET AWAY SCOT-FREE

"As long as everything goes well and nobody deviates from the plan, we should all **GET AWAY WITH THIS HEIST SCOT-FREE.""**

 To suffer no repercussions for your actions.

 Over time, the phrase has been misremembered as "Scott-free" or even "Scotch-free," but the "Scot" was actually an English tax in the 12th century. If you were able to avoid paying your taxes, you'd be Scot-free.

GET COLD FEET

❝I thought you said your friend was going to come rock climbing with us. Don't tell me he **GOT COLD FEET** when he realized we meant we'd be climbing a real mountain.**❞**

MEANING To back out of doing something due to fear or anxiety.

ORIGIN This phrase may stem from an older idiom, first seen in Ben Jonson's 1605 play *Volpone*, in which the title character says "*I am not, as your Lombard proverb saith, cold on my feet.*"

Sometime between 1962 and 1864 a German author, Fritz Reuter, wrote a book called Seedtime and Harvest (in its English translation). In this work, he describes some gamblers who have gathered to play cards. One of them was unwilling to continue playing for fear of losing all his money, and the others made fun of his reticence, "*So, said the Rector*

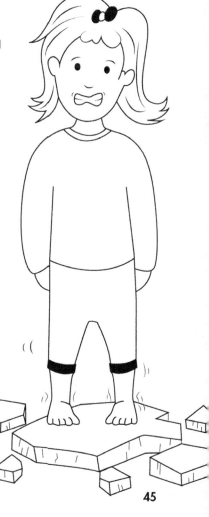

hotly, for he was determined to retain his winnings, "haven't I as good a right to winnings as you? Don't you always get cold feet at our club, when you have had a good luck?" and he carried it out, he kept his cold feet and his winnings."

The phrase appeared again in *The Republican-Journal* of Darlington Wisconsin, in 1805, also – perhaps not surprisingly – in the context of gambling; "*I hastily made up my mind to stay long enough to lose one hundred dollars or so, and then suddenly grow ill and extricate myself. It was a happy thought. 'Cold feet' would pull me out, if my losses became too towering.*"

There is some consensus among researchers that there is a loose association between the poverty of having no shoes and therefore physically cold feet. The expression was first used in an English novel, *Maggie: A Girl of the Streets*, when author, Stephen Crane, wrote "I knew this was the way it would be. They got cold feet." The path of association from poverty, to hopelessness, to nervousness is unclear, however it is interesting to note that during the First World War, men who were hesitant about fighting were called *cold-feeters*.

GET OFF MY BACK

"I'll clean my room when I clean my room. I'm busy today. **GET OFF MY BACK**, Dad.**"**

MEANING Stop reminding, criticizing, bothering, or nagging someone about something.

ORIGIN This saying clearly suggests the imagery of having a weight on your back, or even someone sitting on your back and directing you where to go. Some propose that it is a variation or adaptation of the saying, "to have a monkey on your back," which means to have a problem that someone cannot easily get rid of or solve. "Get off my back" has been in use since the 1800s and has been especially popular since the 1930s.

GET OFF YOUR HIGH HORSE

"You think you're so much better than me just because your mommy buys you brand-name clothes? **GET OFF YOUR HIGH HORSE!** You didn't do anything to earn that stuff."

MEANING Stop acting arrogantly or superiorly.

ORIGIN The first noted use of "high horse" was in John Wyclif's early writings from 1380, in which he said, "*Ye emperour... made hym & his cardenals ride in reed on hye ors.*" Sure, it is spelled a little differently, but the reference is still the same as can be found in our modern expression: that of a very big horse being ridden by a powerful person as a way to show off their power. Whether it was a Roman senator or a medieval landowner, choosing an exceptionally tall horse was a good way to look down on others. The negative use of "high horse" did not come about until the late 1700s or early 1800s, perhaps when people realized that the practice was at least a little ridiculous.

GIVE IT A SHOT

"You'll never know if you could win
if you don't **GIVE IT A SHOT**."

MEANING To make an attempt at something, even if you do not know if you will succeed.

ORIGIN The word "shot" came to mean "try" around the 1800s. Before then, shot only referred to shooting a projectile such as an arrow or a bullet. These days, it is often used to mean to try something new for the first time.

The expressions "take a chance" and "take a leap in the dark" are similar to this.

GIVING (SOMEONE) THE COLD SHOULDER

66 What's with him? All I did was point out that he was in the wrong seat, and he's been **GIVING ME THE COLD SHOULDER** ever since. Why is he acting like such a jerk? 99

MEANING To purposefully ignore or pretend that another person does not exist for the purpose of making your displeasure silently obvious, or to punish them.

ORIGIN In medieval times, visitors were usually met with a literal warm welcome with warm food and a space in front of the fireplace. Unwanted visitors, or those who did not get the hint to leave, would get cold leftovers instead, such as a cold shoulder of mutton.

GO OUT ON A LIMB

❝I'm going to GO OUT ON A LIMB and say that the "genuine bag of stardust" you purchased online for five dollars is probably fake.**❞**

Originally used to introduce a far-out or risky conclusion, but can also be used facetiously to mean a conclusion that is extremely obvious and safe.

This phrase was first recorded in the *Steubenville Daily Herald* in 1895 when describing an election. The paper wrote, "*If we get the 14 votes of Hamilton [County], we've got 'em out on a limb. All we've got to do then is shake it or saw it off.*" The metaphor itself is at least a little older. It stems from the risk that comes with climbing out on thinner and more breakable limbs, away from the strong trunk of a tree.

GOOD GRIEF

"GOOD GRIEF. I just wanted to get home in time for the season finale of my favorite TV show, but it feels as if every single person I know had some emergency they needed my help with. What a pain.**"**

MEANING An expression of mild contempt at the present situation.

ORIGIN "Good grief" comes from the older phrase "Good God," which dates back to the 1600s. Interestingly enough, "good grief" can only be found in writing as early as 1900, from *The English Dialect Dictionary*, and no evidence of it is found in other writing prior to a 1915 issue of *Good Housekeeping* (an American women's magazine).

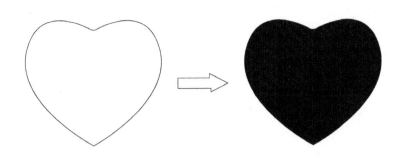

HAVE A CHANGE OF HEART

"My dad was certain he would never adopt a pet, but after fostering a kitten for a little over a month he **HAD A CHANGE OF HEART**, and now we have four cats.**"**

MEANING To change one's mind or opinion.

ORIGIN Although it is similar to the expression "change your mind," there is one key difference. Societies such as the Greeks have associated the heart with emotions for thousands of years. Therefore, to them, to change your heart is to alter your opinion for emotional rather than logical reasons. This idiom has probably existed in some form or another since the 1600s, and it has long been a popular theme in writing, especially romance novels. A classic example of this is Jane Austen's *Pride and Prejudice*, written in 1813. The novel concerns how the main characters Darcy and Elizabeth form hasty and incorrect opinions of each other but each eventually has a change of heart.

HAVE SECOND THOUGHTS

"I know I said I was excited about riding this rollercoaster with you, but I just got hit in the head by one of the bolts that should be holding the tracks together, so now I'm **HAVING SECOND THOUGHTS** about how safe it is...**"**

 To reconsider an original decision.

 This expression is thought to have existed since the 1600s. In 1729 the famous British author Daniel Dafoe (writing under the name Andrew Morton esq.) Wrote a pamphlet entitled *Second Thoughts Are Best*, concerning his suggestions for reform in London to decrease criminality. More than one hundred years later, in 1837, Charles Dickens uses the expression in *The Posthumous Papers of the Pickwick Club*, saying "*On second thoughts, gentlemen, I don't wish you had known him.*"

The logic of the expression is simple to see. A person might have a first thought about a situation, and then have a second thought, or even change of mind, once they had more information. In Britain the plural variation, "on second thoughts," is more common and the singular, "on second thought," is more often used in America.

HiT THE HAY

❝Time to **HIT THE HAY**! We've got a big day tomorrow, so everybody needs to get plenty of sleep tonight!**❞**

 MEANING To go to bed.

ORIGIN For much of human history, hay was the primary bedding material among middle- and lower-income people. The phrase itself came about sometime in the late 1800s or early 1900s, and survived long after the use of straw in mattresses ended.

In 1903, *The Oakland Tribune* contained the first recorded use of the phrase saying "*Sam Berger, the Olympic heavyweight [...] announced that 'he was going to hit the hay.'*" In 1905, *Paxton Sport USA* reported, "*[the baseball player] has a language of his own. Going to bed for him is to 'hit the hay',*" which could indicate that the phrase originated among athletes, before being adopted by the rest of society.

HOLD YOUR HORSES

❝I know you're all hungry, but please **HOLD YOUR HORSES** until all the crew have gotten their food. They need to return to set first, so they have priority over us. I promise you'll all be fed in time.**❞**

 MEANING Wait patiently.

ORIGIN In previous centuries, when most work and travel was accomplished with horses or on horseback, it was important to be skilled in directing horses. Although we might imagine that such an obvious command has been in use for centuries, some believe it only originated in the early 1800s.

New York's Erie canal was first opened for use in 1825, and teams of horses pulled cargo-laden barges along the canal. Usually, more than one team of horses would be in the canal at once. The horse drivers would reportedly occasionally call out to each other to hold their horses, in order to avoid crashes or spooking the horses. The first metaphorical use of this phrase was in the *Warren Democratic Advocate* in 1842; "'*Hold your horses*,' says he, '*and if you want to hear the greatest shaving story that you ever did hear, just keep cool.*'"

HORSE OF A DIFFERENT COLOR

“Language classes have always been easy, but math is a **HORSE OF A DIFFERENT COLOR.** I'm never sure that I'll pass the tests.**”**

 A very different thing or topic.

 In his play *Twelfth Night* (written circa 1601–02), Shakespeare used the phrase implying the opposite meaning: "My purpose is indeed a horse of that colour." By the 1800s, the current idiom had come into use. A different version, "horse of another color," is sometimes used.

Some people claim that in the early days of horse racing people would bet on a horse of a certain color and sometimes one of a different color would win instead. Other people have postulated that, when purebred horses are born, they are registered with careful notes on their coat color and pattern. However, there is no evidence that any of this has anything to do with the idiom.

Similar idioms include "a bird of another feather," "a different breed of cat," and "another can of worms." It is, of course, also similar to "a different kettle of fish."

IN HOT WATER

❝I told you we never should have tried to steal the answer key for the test. If we don't return this, before the teacher notices it is missing, we'll all be **IN HOT WATER.❞**

MEANING In trouble, danger, or an otherwise unpleasant situation.

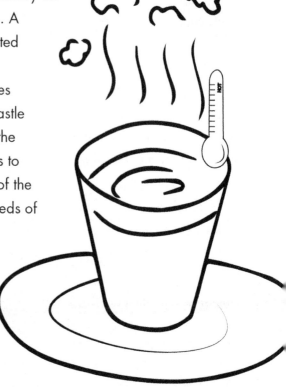

ORIGIN This expression is so old that there is no clear history on its origin and use. A common theory is that it is related to the defense of castles in the 1500s. People would sometimes throw boiling water from the castle walls or out of windows, onto the heads of enemies and intruders to drive them away. This version of the idiom has been used for hundreds of years.

This expression is similar in meaning to "out on a limb," "in a tight spot," and "in a pickle."

IN THE SAME BOAT

66Did every single one of us forget we had a quiz today? Well, at least we're all **IN THE SAME BOAT**...99

 To be in the same predicament or unwelcome situation as another person.

When people are in a small boat together on open water, especially when it is a lifeboat, the status of the people on the boat does not matter. Regardless of gender, wealth, or status, everyone faces the same danger and must work together to survive. This phrase endured, from its very literal meaning in the days of sailing ships. It is often used to deflect accusations of blame or requests for help. Sometimes it is used to express empathy, by showing indicating to someone that you ae or have been in the same situation as them and understand their plight.

IT'S RAINING CATS AND DOGS

❝Why did I have to forget my umbrella today, of all days? **IT'S RAINING CATS AND DOGS!❞**

It is raining really hard and a lot.

The exact origin of this idiom is uncertain. However, the most probably theory is that it relates to animals, primarily cats and dogs, drowning in downpours. Cities such as London had very poor drainage systems in the 1600s, which led to small floods that drowned animals and swept already deceased ones from alleys and into main streets.

The first evidence of this idiom is found in 1951 in the poetry of Henry Vaughan. He writes, *"Themselves with such a roof, that can secure Their wares from dogs and cats rained in shower."* The playwright, Richard Brome, used the phrase, *"It shall raine Dogs and Polecats"* in *City Writ*, which was published in 1653. Jonathan Swift was the first person to place the cat first in the idiom in the 1700s.

Many languages across the world have similarly amusing versions of this idiom. In French they say, "it's raining nails" and "it's raining ropes." In Greek, it "rains chair legs." In Welsh they say, "it's raining knives and forks."

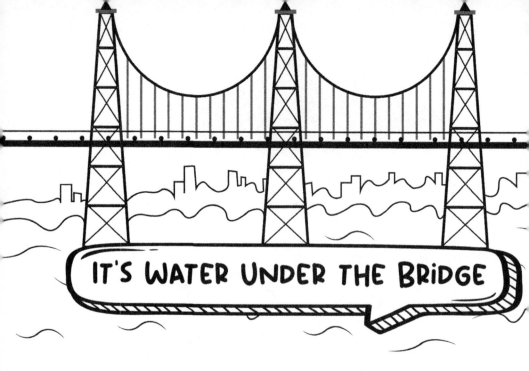

IT'S WATER UNDER THE BRIDGE

"I'm not still mad about what you said the other day, silly! Consider **IT WATER UNDER THE BRIDGE.""**

Something that has already passed and no longer holds any significance, or else cannot be changed and has therefore been accepted.

The earliest example of this phrase can be found in *Dictionnaire de l'Académie Françoise* (1672–1793) in French as *"Laisser passer l'eau sous les ponts,"* or *"to let water flow under the bridge."* The phrase has been found in English as far back as 1844, when *The New Monthly Magazine and Humorist: Part the Third* included it in a piece called *Manzoni*. The title character looks down at the water flowing at his feet and proclaims, *"It has passed under the bridge,"* as he mourns how his life has turned out.

KEEP IT UNDER YOUR HAT

❝ She hasn't told Mom yet, so **KEEP IT UNDER YOUR HAT,** but she's seriously considering accepting an offer to study abroad next year. **❞**

To keep a secret until an appropriate time.

In the 1800s this idiom meant you should keep an idea to yourself, in your brain, i.e. under your hat. Around 1890 its meaning changed in America to keeping something secret. It is speculated that this stems from the then-president of the United States, Abraham Lincoln's keeping important documents inside his hat.

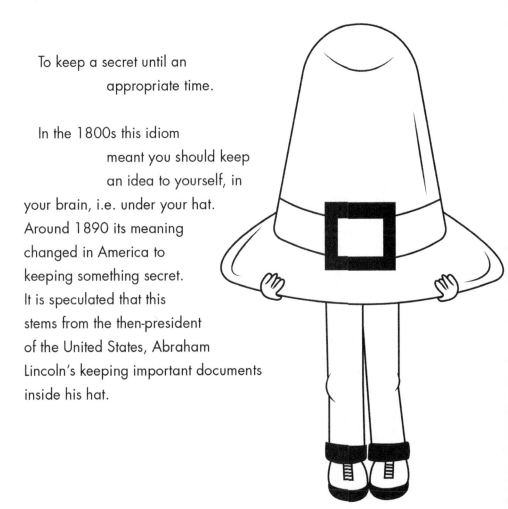

KEEP YOUR SHIRT ON

"KEEP YOUR SHIRT ON, now! He didn't mean to bump into you and even if he did that's no reason to fight.**"**

Calm down.

In the 1800s, when clothing was extremely expensive and hard to replace, men frequently removed their shirts, before engaging in a fight, to avoid damaging them. This is still done to this day, although for many people it is simply because they find wearing a shirt too restrictive or warm if fighting.

KiCK UP YOUR HEELS

❝It's finally the weekend! We can **KICK UP OUR HEELS** and spend the day at the beach.**❞**

To have fun.

ORIGIN Some sources say that this idiom originally meant "to be killed" in the 1600s. That meaning would probably have similar origins as "kick the bucket." The modern meaning came about in the 1900s. It is said to be inspired by the way a horse will prance and gallop when let out into pasture.

KNOCK YOUR SOCKS OFF

"You won't believe the tricks this magician can do. If you have a chance, make sure you catch a show. It will really **KNOCK YOUR SOCKS OFF!"**

To be extremely impressive or astounding.

 Originally, "knock [someone's] socks off" referred to beating or punching somebody so badly in a fight that their socks would fly off of their feet, and the meaning was overwhelmingly threatening. It dates back as far as *Logansport Democratic Pharos's* claim *"the Ague King's American remedy for Chills and Fever, knocks the socks off that disease"* in 1856.

The phrase received its new meaning in the 1960s, when Pepsi-Cola ran an ad campaign to promote their new southern soft drink, Mountain Dew. This drink derived its name from a slang term for moonshine, which is itself a slang term for whiskey. The commercial showcased people from various backgrounds drinking Mountain Dew and then attending events without shoes or socks in order to enjoy "that barefoot feeling," which was considered to be a southern thing. The commercial ended with the line, *"Here's a taste that will just knock your socks off."*

LET ONE'S HAIR DOWN

"Beach days are the best when you need to **LET DOWN YOUR HAIR**. It is useless to worry about appearances and work when you're barefoot on a beach eating quickly melting ice cream.**"**

 MEANING To act freely and without reserve.

ORIGIN In most cultures around the world there have been stretches of hundreds of years when men and women were expected to cover their hair, tie and braid it in specific patterns, cut it in curtain ways, or never cut it at all. Hair has often been connected to a person's modesty, their honor, or their beauty. Typically, it is an indicator of the norms and fashions of a society.

In the 1600s, English women were expected to have long hair that they never cut. However, a modest and proper lady would never have her hair loose in front of anyone but her close family. So, it became fashionable for women to have their hair up in elaborate and stiff hairstyles. It would only be in their homes that they could let it down into a more comfortable style or even leave it loose. Although it gradually became less of a taboo for people outside of the family to see a woman's hair down, the phrase was used literally, up to the 1900s, when it was still fashionable to wear one's hair up.

From the 1920s onwards, the use of the phrase became primarily figurative as women started wearing their hair in bobs.

LET THE CAT OUT OF THE BAG

"Oops, I probably shouldn't have said that. Well, at least now that **THE CAT IS OUT OF THE BAG**, you can help us out with the surprise, right?**"**

 MEANING To reveal something that you can't take back.

ORIGIN There are two predominant theories about where this idiom comes from. The first theorizes that the "cat" is actually the cat o' nine tails, which was a nine-corded whip used as a punishment. The problem with this theory is that the nine-tails is rarely associated with a bag, and is not really considered a surprise or revelation.

The second theory is that in the Middle Ages, merchants might switch out the expensive pig or piglet the customer had just purchased for a cat of no worth. When the buyer arrived home, they would "let the cat out of the bag" and discover the trickery.

The Dutch and German versions of this phrase actually translate directly to "to purchase a cat in a bag." However, neither phrase mentions buying a pig. In fact, Spanish actually has a phrase which translates to "giving a cat instead of a hare." This makes a little more sense, given the difference in weight between cats and pigs. Still, Richard Hill wrote in 1530, "*When ye proffer the pigge open the poke.*" "Poke" was an older word for bag, so perhaps there were merchants out there trading cats for pigs.

Others suggest, and which seems most logical, that the phrase simply came from the difficulty of keeping an upset cat contained within a bag. If you've ever had a cat who dislikes going to the vet, you might have some experience with exactly how fast these guys can run, if they do not like where you've put them.

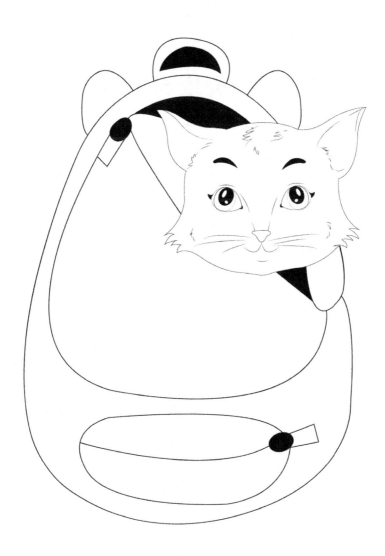

LOSE ONE'S SHIRT

❝You invested how much in that stock?
Bro, haven't you read the papers? The price is dropping
like crazy. You're about to **LOSE YOUR SHIRT!❞**

 MEANING To lose everything financially, down to the clothes on one's back.

 ORIGIN This phrase was first seen around 1935, when America was in the midst of the Great Depression. Many Americans found themselves losing everything they owned because of the stock market crash. It was considered the ultimate sign of poverty to lose even the outfit one was wearing.

MAKE A MOUNTAIN OUT OF A MOLEHILL

"Schools always **MAKE A MOUNTAIN OUT OF A MOLEHILL** about dress code violations. They sent her home for wearing a strappy shirt.**"**

MEANING To make a big deal out of a small issue.

ORIGIN Molehills somewhat resemble tiny mountains of loose ground. Alliteration then probably accounts for the rest of the reason why these two things in particular are compared. Nicolas Udall used this idiom in his 1548 translation of *The First Tome of Volume of the Paraphrase of Erasmus upon the newe testaments*, when he wrote, "*The Sophistes of Grece coulde through their copiousness make an Elephant of a flye, and a mountaine of a mollehill.*" If he did not invent it himself, he at least popularized it.

MAKE A SPLASH

❝ That new movie is **MAKING QUITE A SPLASH**. People are talking about it everywhere, from *The Times* to TikTok. **❞**

 MEANING Make a great impression or quickly gain a lot of attention.

ORIGIN The imagery of drawing attention by jumping into a swimming pool is pretty clear. In fact the artist David Hockney played on this image by calling one of his most famous paintings, A Bigger Splash (1967). However the word splash is thought to be an alteration of the Middle English word *plash*, which meant the same as splash does now. The first use of this expression in its metaphorical sense is found in 1804, however, it has really been more popular since the mid-1900s. A related expression, "making waves," means to have a big impact on the world around one.

MISS THE BOAT

"If we had invested in that electronic company's stock twenty years ago, we'd be rich right now. We really **MISSED THE BOAT** on that one."

 MEANING Miss an opportunity by being too slow or late.

ORIGIN The origin of this phrase is a little unclear, but chances are "miss the boat" began as a literal phrase, in the 18th century, to describe someone who arrived after their ship had left the harbor. Later it became used to describe non-literal occurrences caused by tardiness.

A more recent version, "miss the bus," is said to originate from an 1840 story about an Oxford man, Mark Pattinson. He was meant to visit John Henry Newman, but missed the bus. People believe that he would have had the opportunity to work in the Vatican if he had that conversation with Newman.

MUMBO JUMBO

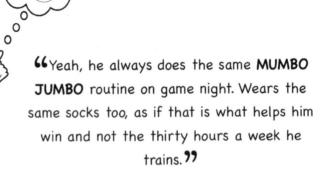

66 Yeah, he always does the same **MUMBO JUMBO** routine on game night. Wears the same socks too, as if that is what helps him win and not the thirty hours a week he trains. 99

MEANING Meaningless nonsense. A ritual or practice that the speaker cannot understand.

ORIGIN This phrase is believed to be a mangling of the name of a Mandingo ancestral figure, *Mama Dyumbo*. Mungo Park used the phrase in his book, *Travels in The Interior of Africa* (1795) when describing a sort of bogeyman figure that is called upon to discipline women when their husbands perceive an affront. He describes a system where a man will don the appearance of the figure and appear at night while making a lot of noise in order to punish the woman in question. Park's disregard for the culture of the people he encountered in his travels is made clear in the way this phrase caught on in Europe. That is people were not concerned with that the origins or original meaning of the phrase was, they merely liked the exotic way to refer to things they considered meaningless or unintelligible.

NIGHT OWL

66Honestly, I'm a real **NIGHT OWL**. I do my best work after midnight. If you ask me to do something that requires a lot of brain power at noon, I'll probably just give up.99

 One who is awake and active during the night rather than the day.

 Most owls are nocturnal, sleeping during the day and hunting at night. However, some are diurnal and are awake during the day. In the 1500s nocturnal owls were called night owls. Shakespeare first used this term to describe a person who preferred the night in his 1594 narrative poem *The Rape of Lucrece*, "… *his guilty hand pluck'd up the latch, And with his knee the door he opens wide. The dove sleeps fast that this night-owl will catch…*".

The expression then became more common in the 1800s.

NOT A HAPPY CAMPER

66If they don't hurry up and feed us soon, I am **NOT GOING TO BE A HAPPY CAMPER.** That wedding took forever. The least they could do is start the reception on time!99

Someone who is having a bad time. Conversely, "happy camper" can be used to describe someone having a good time, but it is rarer.

 There is no definitive origin for this phrase, although the consensus seems to be that it probably was first used to describe children in the popular American custom of sending children off to summer camps. Some speculate that its usage goes back as far as the late 1800s, though others claim it was not used to describe a non-literal camper until 1980. In a 2011 review of Austrian-born composer, Robert Fuchs, Bob McQuiston wrote, "*The piece concludes matter-of-factly in a minor key, leaving one feeling the composer wasn't the "happy camper" he'd once been.*"

Similar expressions include "be down in the dumps," "be blue," or "be bummed."

NOT HAVING A LEG TO STAND ON

"After we were able to show that his lead witness had lied about several key pieces of evidence, the defendant did **NOT HAVE A LEG TO STAND ON** and agreed to settle out of court. **"**

MEANING Being unable to back up one's claims.

ORIGIN When asked how many legs a chair has, you might automatically answer, "four." However, three-legged stools and two-legged leaning chairs were very popular in the past. The fewer legs these chairs had, the less support they would give, and so if a chair's last leg broke, the chair would have "no legs to stand on".

This idiom was already in use in the 1500s, but early examples are hard to source. More recently (2021) the Huffington Post commented on a US politician's speech gaffe, saying *"[Politician's Name], of course, is going to complain loudly when the 'not concerned about the very poor' soundbite is used against him in ads, but he simply has no leg to stand on when it comes to 'context.'"*

ON THIN ICE

"You're **ON THIN ICE**, kid. If you get one more failing grade on a test, you're liable for in-school suspension, and that's not okay.**"**

 MEANING To be extremely close to being in trouble or danger.

 ORIGIN The original form of expression was "skating on thin ice," however the shorter version is a lot more popular these days. This idiom comes from the Netherlands, where people often skate on frozen rivers, ponds, and lakes in winter. If the top layer of the water is not frozen solid, the ice may break and a skater can fall into the water below and drown. Therefore, you are laterally risking your life if you skate on thin ice.

Ralph Waldo Emerson used this phrase in his 1841 essay *Prudence,* "*Iron cannot rust, nor beer sour, nor timber rot, nor calicoes go out of fashion, nor money stocks depreciate, in the few swift moments in which the Yankee suffers any one of them to remain in his possession. In skating over thin ice, our safety is in our speed.*"

OUT OF THE BLUE

OUT OF THE BLUE

"I'm as shocked as you are. I thought for sure we were going to break up, and then **OUT OF THE BLUE** he just asked me to marry him! It was so sudden. I don't really know what to think!**"**

 MEANING Occurring with no prior warning or indication.

ORIGIN The earliest version of this idiom is, "like a bolt out of the clear blue sky." It suggests the unexpectedness and rarity of having thunder and lightning when the sky is seemingly clear of clouds or rain. Thomas Carlyle uses this phrase in his 1837 book, *The French Revolution*, when he describes how French legislation let itself become tangled up, but "… *miraculously a winged Perseus (or Improvised Commune) has dawned out of the void Blue, and cut her loose.*"

The reference to thunder was left off in a 1909 newspaper article when they wrote, "*out of a blue sky.*" By 1979 there was even an American sitcom called "Out of the Blue."

The American idiom "out of left field" has a similar meaning.

OUT OF THE WOODS

"We've still got two more final exams to get through, so don't slack off on your studying tonight. We're not **OUT OF THE WOODS** yet!**"**

 MEANING Free of danger or difficulty.

ORIGIN Although several references I consulted stated that the phrase probably dates back to ancient Rome, none was able to provide an example. Most agreed however, that the phrase was first used in English in the late 1700s. Several sources, particularly, noted that Abigail Adams used the phrase in a letter to Benjamin Franklin; however, as the date of the letter was claimed to be 1800, this is questionable, as Benjamin Franklin died in 1790.

"Out of the woods" is often used in hospitals to say a patient is or is not likely to pass away.

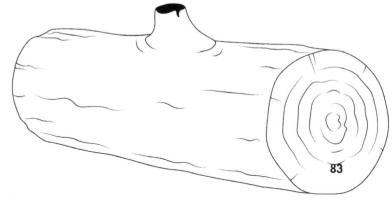

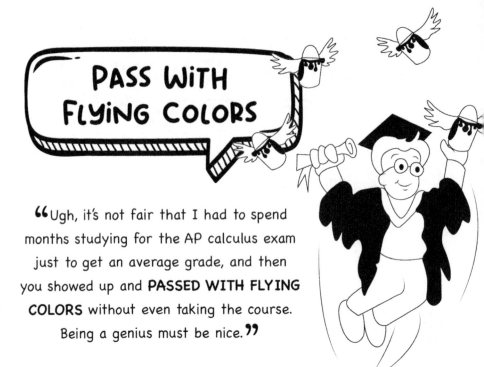

PASS WITH FLYING COLORS

"Ugh, it's not fair that I had to spend months studying for the AP calculus exam just to get an average grade, and then you showed up and **PASSED WITH FLYING COLORS** without even taking the course. Being a genius must be nice."

MEANING Get a fantastic grade on a course, test, or assignment.

ORIGIN As far back as the 1500s, sailing ships flew flags to show the country they came from. They also slowly developed a system of using other flags to communicate with other ships. This gives us the image of a ship passing another, with all its colors (flags) flying, showing who it was and, therefore, passing the unstated "identification test".

"Colors" is also slang for uniforms, flags, and other visual indicators of which country or clan a group of people belong. When a ship won a sea battle, it would often arrive in its home port with all its flags proudly flying in celebration. If a ship was defeated, the sailors would leave the flags at half-mast. The figurative use of this phrase started in the 1700s.

PAY THROUGH THE NOSE

"Our dresses looked nearly identical.
I got mine from a chain store, but she
PAID THROUGH HER NOSE for a name brand.**"**

MEANING To pay an outrageous amount for something, especially if the price is exorbitant.

ORIGIN One dubious theory states that the Danes placed a tax on Ireland in the 9th century and cut off the noses of all those who could not pay.

Another version makes a connection between the Greek word for nose, 'Rhinos', and 17th century slang for money, 'Rhino'. Rhino horn and other body parts are notoriously in demand on the black market and thus very expensive.

This idiom appears in an Italian book of proverbs, *Piazza universale di proverbi Italiani0* (A common place of Italian proverbs and proverbial phrases) written in 1666, by Giovanni Torriano). He said, "*Oft-times Rich men engrossing commodities, will make one pay through the nose, whereas they might sell the cheaper.*"

The English version was then used by English poet and politician Andrew Marvell in 1678 when he said, "*When they came to seek for Match, and Bullet, and Powder, there was none to be had. The Fanaticks had bought it all up, and made them pay for it most unconscionably, and through the Nose.*"

PLAY IT BY EAR

"Between your schedule and mine, the only time that really seems to work is next Tuesday—as long as your meeting is canceled—so let's **PLAY IT BY EAR** until we know for sure."

MEANING To avoid making definitive plans with the intention of figuring things out at a later time, or to improvise.

ORIGIN This expression originated in reference to the ability to play a piece of music without having ever looked at its paper score. By the 1930s, the expression had changed to cover anything that was done without a solid plan. Since the original saying referred to an ability to reproduce a certain song by listening, the expression may have changed meaning when the concept of improvisation became popular among jazz musicians. By listening to one another, a band could create a brand-new piece of music "by ear", live on stage.

PULL SOMEONE'S LEG

"You really said that? Out loud? You're **PULLING MY LEG!**
There's no way that actually happened."

 To kid around with someone, lie in a joking manner, or attempt to prank someone by presenting something absurd as completely true.

Truth be told, we really have no idea where this phrase came from! It is suspected that the origin might have something to do with the practice of thieves in the marketplace, of pulling on somebody's leg in order to trip them so they could be robbed, but every version of this story changes the time and location where this may have hypothetically taken place. Some sources believe the phrase to be of Scottish origin, others British, and others American. We do know that the phrase can be found in its Scottish form in William Anderson's 1851 novel *Rhymes, Reveries, and Reminiscences* as "*He preached, an' at last drew the auld body's leg,*" in reference to a man cheating an old woman out of her money. The phrase can be found in its full modern form not once but twice in an anonymously published 1859 novel called *Always Ready, or, Every One his Pride*. Firstly, "*Both brothers commenced "pulling his leg" by criticising his rig [= outfit]...*" and then "*I know you are pulling my leg,*" continued he, "*but I'll tell you candidly what it is, Harry—we shall both miss you.*"

In 1914, a descendant of American banker, James Gallatin, published what were advertised to be his diaries, including an 1821 entry which contained the line "*I really think father, in a covert way, pulls his leg,*" which would arguably be the earliest use of the phrase, in wiring, This but for the fact that the diary is largely considered to be fake and the entries made up. Perhaps James Gallatin really did use the idiom back in 1821, or perhaps his descendant was just pulling our legs!

PUT A BUG IN SOMEONE'S EAR

66 The teacher **PUT A BUG IN OUR EAR** about a possible quiz next week. 99

 MEANING To give someone a hint or make a suggestion.

 ORIGIN This is apparently an American idiom which took its roots from a French saying, dating from the 1300s. The French meaning was, however, somewhat different, and was taken from a translation of the writings of a French Cistercian monk called Guillaume de Deguileville. This monk used the expression to say describe how man's emotions could be stirred by great wonders. How the idiom came to America from France remains a mystery. The oldest mention I could find was a 1975 academic paper about idioms, but even then, it is only very briefly mentioned.

This idiom is sometimes confused with the English saying, "put a flea in one's ear," (which was also a derivative of de Deguileville 's writing) which means to scold someone.

RAIN ON SOMEONE'S PARADE

❝Look, we all know that he's not probably to win the writing contest, but there's no reason to tell him that while we're celebrating the fact that he was able to submit his entry in time! Why do you feel the need to **RAIN ON HIS PARADE?**❞

 MEANING Make a negative or disheartening comment when someone is celebrating.

ORIGIN Although it gained popularity through the song *Don't Rain on My Parade* in the 1964 musical *Funny Girl*, this idiom has existed since the early 1900s at the very least. In 1912, the *Schenectady Gazette* ran a story in which a male hunter lamented to his buddies that some woman *"would show up to 'rain on the parade',"* meaning that she would ruin the trip for the rest of them.

READ BETWEEN THE LiNES

Read

" Dude, if you **READ BETWEEN THE LINES** of what she's saying, it's obvious she has a crush on you! Don't be so literal. **"**

MEANING Look deeper into what's being said or written to understand the true meaning, intended by the speaker or writer.

ORIGIN Cryptology is a process where people study, write, and solve codes. People generally write in code to send secret information to one another. Sometimes people other than the intended will try to steal the message and figure out the code. In the 1800s, one method of sending a secret coded message was to write the secret message in between the lines of the main message. The secret message would be written in invisible ink that could be read by heating the message over a flame.

The first figurative use of this idiom was in 1862 in *The New York Times*; "... *the letter assumes a somewhat enigmatical character, and the only resource we have is, as best we may, to "read between the lines" of this puzzling, but important, communication of the British Foreign Secretary...*"

RULE OF THUMB

❝As a **RULE OF THUMB**, I try to wave to someone
when they're between ten and twenty feet from me,
and then verbally greet them when we're around five feet apart.
That keeps things from being awkward, like when
I say 'hi' too early, and they don't hear me.❞

MEANING A general, non-specific standard that most people agree on, or that is relied on due to prior experience.

ORIGIN Throughout history, most measurements were based on the human body. The rule of thumb comes from the days before standardized measurements, when the easiest thing you had measure with was literally on your hand. However, ever since the 1600s this idiom has developed to mean a rough estimation of a situation or behavior, rather than just a rough estimation of a measurement.

SAVING (SOMETHING) FOR A RAINY DAY

"You know what I want to eat? That extra special chocolate bar I bought a few months ago that I've been **SAVING FOR A RAINY DAY.** **"**

 MEANING To save (something) up just in case of bad times.

 ORIGIN A rainy day here is meant to represent gloom and misfortune. The earliest use of this idiom was in an Italian play, *La Spiritata*, by A. F. Grazzini, written in mid-1561. In England, it was used by Nicholas Breton in 1582, in his *Works*, "*Wise men say keepe somewhat till a rainy day.*"

BEST CHOICE

SECOND TO NONE

66Ever since my brother finished culinary school, his creme brulées have been **SECOND-TO-NONE**. I can't order them in restaurants anymore because they're just not as good as his are!99

 MEANING The absolute best of the best.

 ORIGIN If you are not second, you are first. This phrase goes about saying it in a slightly confusing way, but probably better than saying, "You're first!" The expression was first used around 1590 by Shakespeare in his play, *The Comedy of Errors*, when the character Angelo says, "*Of very reverend reputation, sir, Of credit infinite, highly beloved, Second to none that lives here in the city: His word might bear my wealth at any time.*"

SEE EYE TO EYE

"I want to go to the concert with my friends, but my weird dad wants to go fishing. He just doesn't get how important this is to me, no matter how hard I try to explain. The two of us never **SEE EYE TO EYE.""**

 To understand or sympathize with another person.

 This phrase first appears in the Christian Bible, *in Isaiah, 52:8: "Or they shall see eye to eye, when the Lord shall bring again Zion."* Its meaning here is a bit more literal, as it refers to people meeting face-to-face. The shift from literally to figuratively is from looking each other in the eye to mentally meeting each other on the same level.

SHAKE A LEG

"SHAKE A LEG, kids! We're leaving in less than ten minutes. Those fish aren't going to catch themselves. **"**

MEANING Hurry up!

ORIGIN Some evidence suggests that this phrase dates back to the American Civil War, where paramedics shook the leg of an injured soldier to determine if he was still alive. Other sources posit that the phrase originated with sailors as "show a leg." When ships came into port, the sailors were not allowed to leave it, so their wives (or other women) would come aboard to keep them company. When it came time to work, the crew master might call "show a leg" to determine which human-shaped lumps were men who needed to work, versus women who were allowed to continue sleeping.

Or again, the phrase might refer to the act of dancing, as we can see similarities between this and "shake a toe" or "shake a tail feather."

SITTING PRETTY

❝She won the lottery,
so she's **SITTING PRETTY** in a new house,
with a fancy car and some smart investments.**❞**

MEANING To be in a comfortable and secure position.

ORIGIN This idiom comes from the rich slang of early 1900s America. The imagery it invokes is of someone sitting in a raised chair above other people. It was the title of two musicals, in 1921 and 1924, respectively. There was also a popular song, called "I'm Sitting Pretty in a Pretty Little City" that came out in 1923.

Some similar idioms include "Being on top of the world," "Being ahead of the game," and "Being on cloud nine."

SLIP ONE'S MIND

"Oh, you're kidding. The bake sale was today? It must have completely **SLIPPED MY MIND.** I don't have anything prepared!**"**

MEANING To have forgotten about something, usually a small thing, entirely.

ORIGIN The imagery of this idiom is clear, with something not catching in the mind. An older version is, "it slipped out of my mind," but this version is seldom used today. The oldest written use of "slipped my mind" that I could find was in Thomas Miner's *Letter on the Cholera*, which appears in an American journal in 1832, and which says, *"I cannot think of everything at once, and shall therefore be troubling you frequently with letters, so long as the subject of cholera commands an interest, making queries upon matter which has previously slipped my mind."*

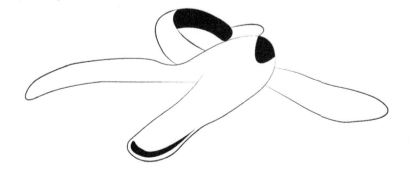

SOMETHING UP ONE'S SLEEVE

66You are looking very smug today, what trick do you have **UP YOUR SLEEVE?99**

 **MEANING** To have a hidden advantage or secret backup plan.

ORIGIN This is related to three older expressions. The first one, "a trick up one's sleeve," dates back to the 1500s, when people had very long and large sleeves that served as pockets. Later on, magicians would also hide things in their sleeves, that allowed them to carry out their tricks.

The other two expressions; "a card up one's sleeve" and "an ace up your sleeve" are related to card games. In the 1800s, people would often play card games and bet money on winning. Some less honest people would cheat by hiding an advantageous card in their sleeve to help them win. In poker, especially, the card would regularly be an ace, because that is the most valuable card in poker and similar games.

100

SPEAK ONE'S MIND

❝This community meeting is a safe space for everyone, so feel free to **SPEAK YOUR MIND!**❞

 Say what you want to say.

 This expression was first recorded in William Shakespeare's *As You Like It*, written in 1599, with the line *"Give me leave to speak my mind,"* although it is very probable that the phrase is much, much older.

Similar expressions include "Speak your own mind," "Let your voice be heard," and "Say your piece."

SPILL THE BEANS

66 So, what did he say when you asked him about the date? Come on now, **SPILL THE BEANS!** 99

 MEANING Reveal a secret or share gossip.

ORIGIN There is an elaborate tale of white and black beans being used to vote on allowing new applicants into a guild in Ancient Greece. The members of a guild would supposedly place a white bean into a container to vote yes, and black to vote no. Only the vote counters were meant to see how many negative votes there were. However, occasionally the container would spill and everyone would see the vote that should have been secret. However, as always, doubt exists as to whether this is actually true.

Regardless, it is this story that is referenced when the phrase was used in 1908 in an American journal, *The Stevens Point Journal*, in June 1908, and again in 1911 in a newspaper, *The Van Wert Daily Bulletin*. Both cases concerned politicians admitting to hidden information. The more general and casual use of the phrase continued from that time onwards.

STICK ONE'S NECK OUT

"I repeatedly defended her to our mom, despite how much I got yelled at, and it turns out she was guilty all along. That's the last time I will **STICK MY NECK OUT** for her.**"**

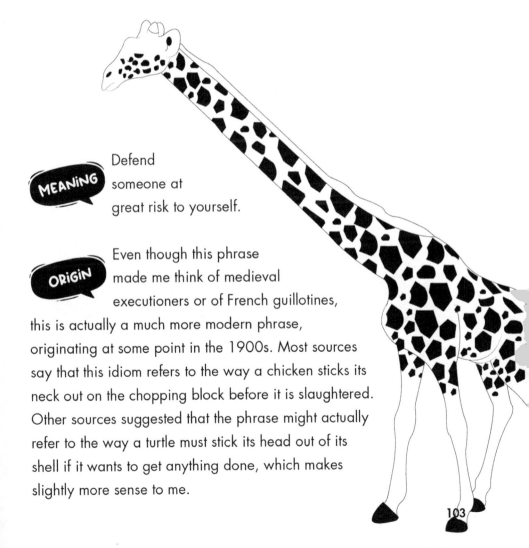

MEANING Defend someone at great risk to yourself.

ORIGIN Even though this phrase made me think of medieval executioners or of French guillotines, this is actually a much more modern phrase, originating at some point in the 1900s. Most sources say that this idiom refers to the way a chicken sticks its neck out on the chopping block before it is slaughtered. Other sources suggested that the phrase might actually refer to the way a turtle must stick its head out of its shell if it wants to get anything done, which makes slightly more sense to me.

STiR THE HORNET'S NEST

❝He **STIRRED UP A HORNET'S NEST** when he accused his brother's dog of eating his shoes. Their mom almost sent them and their dogs all away. **❞**

Purposefully making a commotion or causing trouble.

 'Stir' here does not mean dipping a spoon in a nest, but rather to waking something up.

Hornets often make their nests in places such as roofs, where they are easily disturbed by humans going about their business around the nests. The creatures can be fairly aggressive and may sting repeatedly, which makes them dangerous. Most people learn to be careful not to bother them out of fear of being attacked. This makes for fairly clear and vivid imagery.

The earliest use of this idiom is in Latin. Plautus, a Roman playwright, uses it in his work *Amphitruo*, from around the time of 200 BCE, when the character, Sosia, counsels Amphitryon not to make trouble for himself by quarreling with his wife.

"Amphitruo: ... *quae me hodie advenientem domum noluerit salutare. (Humour her? By the Lord, it will be bad humour, that's sure,—arriving home to-day and she unwilling to give me a decent welcome!)Sosia. Inritabis crabrones. (You'll be poking up a hornet's nest.)*"

The English history of this idiom is not clear. However, it was used in novels dating back to the 1700s. The idioms "open a can of worms" and "rock the boat" are somewhat similar to this.

STRAIGHT FROM THE HORSE'S MOUTH

"I'm not lying! I heard it **STRAIGHT FROM THE HORSE'S MOUTH.** We're going to have a quiz tomorrow. The teacher totally slipped up and told me to my face.**"**

 MEANING Gaining information directly from the perpetrator, the person most involved or the best informed about a thing.

ORIGIN This was originally part of horse racing slang. It comes from the fact that horse sellers might say a horse is younger than it really is to sell it at a higher price. Horse buyers would look at the wear and tear of the horse's teeth to determine whether the seller was telling the truth. A horse is also guided through a bit that is placed in their mouth. If a horse was mistreated by a previous owner, its mouth might have sores, scars, hardened skin, or other injuries to indicate this. A poorly trained or mistreated horse will often behave poorly. No matter what a seller says about the condition and temperament of a horse, an experienced buyer can look at the horse's mouth and see the truth.

SWEAT LIKE A PIG

❝I forgot how miserable theme parks are in August. The rides are refreshing, sure, but standing in these queue lines had me **SWEATING LIKE A PIG.❞**

 MEANING To sweat profusely.

 ORIGIN Interestingly enough, though we can all picture a dripping porker in our minds, pigs actually lack the eccrine glands necessary to produce sweat. They do still possess apocrine glands which cause an odor, but they use mud and water to cool themselves down.

There's a theory that the term actually refers to a step in the iron-smelting process in which oblong chunks of metal are poured onto sand and left to cool. Since the 15th century, these pieces have been called *sows*, and eventually became *pigs* in the 16th century. As the

pig cools, the metal reaches a dew-point and beads of sweat form on its surface.

Other sources point out that the phrase has too widespread a popularity to have originated in such a niche field, since the idiom was used in *The Morning Post* in 1824, and had probably been around for a long time beforehand.

A similar phrase also exists in Italian, *"sudare com' un porco,"* which was popular at the same time as the English version's first publication, although no substantial connections were made between the two.

TAKE IT WITH A GRAIN OF SALT

❝He acts as if he knows everything about superheroes, but he's never even read a comic. If he tries to tell you you're not a 'real' fan, based on which characters you like, **TAKE HIS OPINION WITH A PINCH OF SALT.❞**

 MEANING Do not believe someone or something too easily.

 ORIGIN A grain is a now-outdated measurement that was equal to about roughly 0.002 ounces. One teaspoon can hold about 0.08 ounces of salt.

It is thought that this idiom comes from people either taking small amounts of salt as medicine, or taking medicine with some salt to supposedly help improve the taste.

The Roman author, Pliny the Elder, used the phrase, *"after having added a grain of salt"* in his *Naturalis Historia*, which was first published in 77 BCE. The salt was part of an antidote to poison.

A Roman general called Pompey, who lived between 106 and 48 BCE, is said to have believed that if he took small amounts of poison every day, he would become immune to poisoning. (There is no proof that this worked.) He is said to have swallowed the poison with a grain of salt to make it go down more easily. If salt made the poison taste better, then the poison must have truly been disgusting!

However, anything written about or by either of these figures would have been in Latin, and it is useful to know that the Latin word, *"sal,"* means both salt and wit. Wit means clever or quick-thinking. So, maybe they were just warning people to take either poison or its antidote with 'wit' and not actual salt.

Despite most of the above history leading to the phrase's being used in England, this version of the idiom is most popular in America. The English tend to say, "take it with a pinch of salt" instead. Indeed, "a grain of salt" was first used, figuratively, in an American literary magazine, *The Athenaeum*, in 1908, when they said, *"Our reasons for not accepting the author's pictures of early Ireland without many grains of salt."*

The "a pinch of salt" version seems to be more common in Great Britain and was used in 1948 by English author, F. R. Cowell, in his work *Cicero & the Roman Republic*, written in 1948, where he said, *"A more critical spirit slowly developed, so that Cicero and his friends took more than the proverbial pinch of salt before swallowing everything written by these earlier authors."*

TAKE THE BULL BY THE HORNS

"Just **TAKE THE BULL BY THE HORNS** and
tell her she is being a bully.**"**

 Deal with a problem directly.

ORIGIN In Spanish bullfights, the banderillas would sometimes
literally grab bulls by their horns to push their heads
down and tire them out. A Spanish proverb is based on
this, *"Take a bull by its horns and a man by his word,"* and may have
been taken up and shortened by English speakers. An early example
of the phrase in print appeared in an 1873 article in the *New York
Times*, entitles *A Brave Policeman A Mad Bull Seized by the Horns.*

TEACHER'S PET

❝I swear, every time the whole class gets in trouble, she magically finds a way to avoid being punished. She's such a **TEACHER'S PET.❞**

MEANING A student who is heavily favored by the teacher.

ORIGIN Despite searching far and wide, I was not able to find any information on the origin of this phrase beyond that it may have been published for the first time in the 1890s. The only thing we can say for sure is that it almost certainly originated among school children at some point, before that time. Interestingly enough, I also could not find any information on when classroom pets first appeared.

Therefore, I have no idea whether the derogatory phrase took its inspiration from a real classroom pet, or if it came before the introduction of animals into the classroom.

112

THE BALL IS IN YOUR COURT

“Look, I've given you all the information and told you everything I know. If you want to do something about it, **THE BALL IS IN YOUR COURT.**”

MEANING If you want things to continue, you will need to be the one to make the next move.

ORIGIN This idiom comes from tennis, which was invented in 1873. You probably know that this game is played on a tennis court, which is divided in two by a net. If your opponent hits the ball, it is allowed to bounce once on your side of the court. If you do not hit the ball before it bounces a second time, your opponent wins a point. Once the ball is on your side, neither your opponent nor anyone else can control what happens to the ball. What happens next is entirely up to you, you hit the ball back or you miss your chance. The figurative use of this expression really only started in the 1960s, for example when Forbes magazine printed the expression "The ball is in your court to take your career to the next level."

THE BEST OF BOTH WORLDS

❝I thought I would have to choose between spending the holidays with my family or with my friends.
Then Addy said he could give me a lift just after Christmas.
So, I will spend a week with my family and a week with my friends. It's **THE BEST OF BOTH WORLDS!❞**

MEANING Having multiple good things/options, where one would normally expect to sacrifice one comfort for another.

ORIGIN As far as we know, the earliest form of this idiom was used by the French author Voltaire in his 1759 novel, *Candide*. He used the phrase *"the best of all possible worlds"*. Some suggest that the version we are familiar with came into being in the mid-1800s and only became more popular in the late 1900s. The two worlds originally referenced by this idiom may be "this life" and the "afterlife." The historic, or religious meaning would then be that someone is living a happy and comfortable life while being moral enough that they are assumed to be guaranteed the best after life, as promised by their religion.

A similar expression is "it's a win-win situation."

THE ICING ON THE CAKE

66Their holiday trip was already a great deal of fun; the fact that it snowed on the last day was just **THE ICING ON THE CAKE.**99

MEANING Something extra that makes something, which is already good, even better.

ORIGIN Surprisingly, cakes have been around for thousands of years. Icing and toppings, however, are a more recent invention. A type of icing did exist in 1494, but it was only used on a specific sort of cookie. One hundred and sixty years later, in 1655, a woman called Rebecca Price reportedly had some iced cakes made. It is odd then that the English author Elizabeth Raffald is credited with inventing icing and frosting in 1769. Regardless, she was the first to publish a recipe for icing. It is believed that the use of the idiom only started after the publication of her recipe book.

The first metaphorical use of the phrase in writing appeared in 1889, in an early science fiction story, by American author, Howard Fielding, called *The Automatic Bridget*.

THE WORLD IS YOUR OYSTER

"That's the only store you want to go into in this whole shopping center? Come on, man! **THE WORLD IS YOUR OYSTER**! What else do you want to do?"

 You can have or do anything you want without restrictions.

 This phrase was first seen in William Shakespeare's play, *The Merry Wives of Winsor*. The character, Pistol, answers, "*Why then the world's mine oyster, Which I with sword will open,*" in response to the character, Falstaff's, asking him to lend hum a penny. It should be noted that Shakespeare is credited with the creation of hundreds of words and phrases.

However, some historians believe it may simply be the case that Shakespeare was merely the first person to put popular, lower-class slang into writing.

The origin of the metaphorical meaning is a little unclear. It is suggested that an oyster relates to being rich. This would then metaphorically shift to mean being rich in life's opportunities.

THROUGH THICK AND THIN

"What did I tell you? We always stick together. We'll be there for you **THROUGH THICK AND THIN**, no matter what.**"**

MEANING To support someone equally well, through good and bad times.

ORIGIN This idiom comes from the old hunting expression "through the thicket and thin woods," and was shortened over time. It was difficult to get through thick, bushed areas, but hunting in sparse woods was easier, so the hunt could go through more easily. The idiom even appears in *The Canterbury Tales* (1387–1400), specifically in The Reeve's tale, when Chaucer says, "*When the said horse was free and saw his chance, Toward the fen, for wild mares ran therein, And with a 'whinny' he went, through thick and thin.*"

THROW IN THE TOWEL

"There's no way I can win this eating contest with my stomach acting up like this. I might as well just **THROW IN THE TOWEL** now and save myself the hospital trip."

MEANING To quit or to admit defeat.

ORIGIN During a boxing match, the fighters' coaches or seconds would keep a towel on hand to wipe sweat from the fighter's face between rounds. When one fighter was unable to continue, the coach or second would throw the towel into the ring to signify that the opponent had won. The first recorded use of the phrase comes from the *Kalgoorlie Western Argus* in 1900: "*Sullivan was beaten out, his second throwing in the towel.*" The *Sunday Times* used it figuratively just three years later to describe a mayoral election.

FUN FACT The phrase "throw in the sponge" was actually used for many years before "throw in the towel." Boxers originally used sponges to mop their brow and to signify giving up in exactly the way they would later use towels. "*Throw in the sponge*" was even defined in *The Slang Dictionary* of 1860.

The expressions "wave a white flag," "jump ship,", "bow out," and "cut and run" all also relate to quitting a situation.

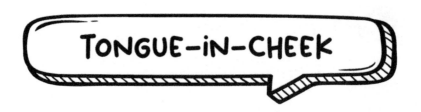

TONGUE-IN-CHEEK

"This old man was being very rude at the museum,
so my friend agreed with him, **TONGUE IN CHEEK**,
that teens these days spend too much time on their phones. She
then used her phone to take a photo of the QR code and
read the online exhibition guide aloud to me.**"**

MEANING As with sarcasm, this is when something is said in a seemingly serious way, but is really meant as a joke.

 ORIGIN This phrase originally meant to show disdain, and described how someone would physically put their tongue in their cheek to show disrespect for someone else or an idea. In 1748, Tobias Smollet published his book *The Adventures of Roderick Ransom*. Roderick takes a coach to Bath and on the way they're set upon by a highway man. Roderick says, *"I signified my contempt of him by thrusting my tongue in my cheek, which humbled him so much, that he scarce swore another oath aloud during the whole journey."*

The expression began to approach the meaning that we use today nearly a century later and in the 1800s it had changed to the expression we use today. In 1828, Sir Walter Scott used the expression in his novel, *The Fair Maid of Perth*, to mean suppressed amusement; such as biting one's tongue to stop from bursting out laughing; *"The fellow who gave this all-hail thrust his tongue in his cheek to some scapegraces like himself."*

UNDER THE WEATHER

"Are you feeling okay? You've been looking a bit **UNDER THE WEATHER** all day. Would you like to go to the nurse's office?**"**

 MEANING To be sick, sad, or gloomy.

ORIGIN A few centuries ago, *under* did not always mean to physically be beneath or below something. It sometimes meant "affected by." So, the original meaning of this idiom would be that someone was being influenced by the weather. Since the days of the earliest ships and still today, people can get seasick, or motion-sick, when they sail on a ship. If it is stormy or the seas are rough, a ship will roll and dip in ways which make people nauseous and dizzy. This means that people literally become sick due to the weather.

WALK ON EGGSHELLS

❝I love hanging out with her when she's in a good mood, but I swear, sometimes I feel as if I'm **WALKING ON EGGSHELLS** around her. She'll snap at the slightest suggestion of a criticism, even if I didn't mean anything by it.**❞**

 To treat something with extreme caution.

 When collecting eggs in the early morning, farmers would be careful not to step on eggs or eggshells that could make a lot of noise and bother the hens. The idiom has been in use since the 1500 as sometime between 1544–1587, The writer George Whetstone wrote a play, called "*The rocke of regard divided into foure parts…*" In this he said , "*they come to the point it self, then lo, they treade so nicely and gingerly, as though they walked vpon eggs and feared they breaking of them.*"

This idiom is similar to "walking on thin ice."

WET BLANKET

"Look, I don't want to be a **WET BLANKET**, but if we don't start winding up this party, the neighbors will absolutely report a noise complaint.**"**

MEANING To dampen or stop other people's fun or enjoyment.

ORIGIN It was common practice from around the 1660s onwards for cooks to keep a wet blanket in the kitchen. This was used to quickly put out fires. The expression was first used figuratively in a newspaper, *The Kentish Gazette*, in 1798, when the paper said, "*There was no man so besotted as to not believe that the Swiss would heartily join in the cause, if a general confederacy was formed on the Continent. But if this motion were to be adopted, we should throw a wet blanket on the fire, which was otherwise about to spread through Europe.*"

There are a few other fun expressions that refer to the type of person that is not known for being the life of the party. These include "fuddy-duddy," "goody two-shoes," "stick-in-the-mud," and "Grinch."

WHEN PIGS FLY

"You'll finish remodeling the basement **WHEN PIGS FLY**. Seriously, you've been "working on it" for twenty years. Why don't you just hire a contractor?"

 MEANING Something that's never going to happen.

 ORIGIN The idiom itself dates back to as far as the 1600s, although it is not known whether it came from an older Scottish saying or a German one. In fact, numerous cultures around the world have ideologically similar sayings to express the impossibility of an outcome. They all begin with "when–" and mention an animal doing something it could never do. Examples are, *"when hens have teeth"* from the French, the very odd *"when the crayfish whistle on the mountain"* from Russian, and *"until the donkey ascends the ladder"* from Hebrew.

Some other English idioms about impossibilities include "to find a needle in a haystack," "to catch lighting in a bottle," and "on the first of never."

WAKE UP ON THE WRONG SIDE OF THE BED

❝Looks like somebody **WOKE UP ON THE WRONG SIDE OF THE BED** today. What's with the sour expression?**❞**

MEANING To look gloomy or be bad-tempered, as though you had a terrible night's sleep.

ORIGIN This phrase appeared as a counterpart to the original notion of getting up on the 'right' side of the bed—and they actually meant *right*, as in the opposite of *left*. In Ancient Rome, the left side of all things was considered unlucky, so getting up on the right side of the bed with your right foot first was important for ensuring a safe and lucky day.

Interestingly, the Roman word for left was *sinistra*, and this gradually became sinister with its modern meaning solidifying around the 15th century. When Shakespeare wrote *Hamlet*, he had Hamlet hold the skull of his old court jester, Yorick, in his left hand signifying the unlucky aspect of the gesture!

An older form of the idiom, "get out of bed on the wrong side," is seldom used these days.

WOLF IN SHEEP'S CLOTHING

"He is a **WOLF IN SHEEP'S CLOTHING.**
He said he would help us with the science project,
but then stole it and submitted it with his friends.**"**

 Someone who hides their true character by pretending to be the opposite, and who would harm you if they had the opportunity.

 an ancient Latin proverb says *"Pelle sub agnina latitat mens saepe lupina (Under a sheep's skin often hides a wolfish mind)"* meaning something much more evil may lurk under a seemingly innocent surface.

The Christian Bible also has a similar phrase when Jesus speaks in Matthew 7:15: *"Watch out for false prophets. They come to you in sheep's clothing, but inwardly they are ferocious wolves."* our modern idiom probably developed from one or both of these sources and was then popularized through various fables, most notably Aesop's story, *A Wolf in Sheep's Clothing.*

CONCLUSION

And there we are; 101 sayings! They are barely a fraction of all the sayings we have in English. How many of these sayings did you already know? I bet more than you thought you did.

Now that you know that phrases, such as "a wet blanket" and "get away scot-free", once described parts of the daily lives of people who lived 400 years ago. The number of idioms that concern animals, especially cats and horses, shows just how much people relied on and centered their lives around their animals in the past. All the new sayings that came about in the 1900s speak to the way the new inventions and rapid changes of this century have affected our world and how we talk about it.

Many of the sayings suggest something about the influence that writers, such as Chaucer and Shakespeare, had on us through their works. It is also interesting to see how music played a role in spreading idioms in the last 100 or so years. The idioms we use today link us to those other humans, who lived hundreds of years ago. Thus we see that our language is a living history of us and a link to all humankind.

Can you imagine which examples of today's slang will live on as idioms and expressions? I can't wait to see.